ROCKS AND MINERALS

Cally Oldershaw

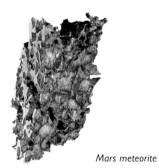

Mars meteorite

A Golden Photo Guide from St. Martin's Press

Mica biotite

Geode

Silicon chip

Gneiss

Amethyst crystals

ROCKS AND MINERALS

A Golden Photo Guide from St. Martin's Press

St. Martin's Press
New York
Manufactured in China

Produced by
Elm Grove Books Limited
Series Editor Susie Elwes
Text Editor Angela Wilkes
Art Director Louise Morley
Illustration John Woodcock
Index Hilary Bird

Original Edition © 1999
Image Quest Limited
This edition © 2002
Elm Grove Books Ltd
Text and Photographs in this book
previously published in
Eyewitness 3D Rocks and Minerals

St. Martin's Press
175 Fifth Avenue
New York, N.Y. 10010
www.stmartins.com

A CIP catalogue record for this
book is available from the
Library of Congress

ISBN 0-312-28921-9

This edition published 2002
A Golden Guide ® is a registered
trademark of Golden Books Publishing
Company, Inc. A Golden Photo Guide
from St. Martin's Press is used
under the terms of a license of that
registered trademark

ACKNOWLEDGMENTS
Photographic Credits
AKG, London: 29br, 30br, 33tl, 39tl, 49br; Bridgeman Art Library: 31bl; British Museum: 40 l; De Beers: 44r, 46bl; WernerForman Archive: 33l, 39c, 40 br, 41bl, 41br; Geoscience Features; 7bc, 14br, 15bl, 20tl 23tr, 24b, 25tl, 27bl, 38br, 42bl, 43bl; Pierre Gideon 9c, 27c ; Hutchinson Library: 26tl; Robert Harding: 4bl, 5 br, 11bl, 11br, 14tl, 16br, 25br, 44 l, 46tl; NASA: 53bl; David McCarthy: 47; Natural History Museum, London: 4br, 6bl, 7bll, 10tl, 13br, 15tl, 15br, 17bl, 17tr, 19bl, 19br, 20br, 21bl, 22b, 23br, 24tl, 25bll, 26bl, 26r, 27tl, 27br, 28tl, 28b, 29bl, 31br, 32l, 32r, 34, 35tl, 3b, 36br, 37cl, 37bl, 37br, 39br, 41tl, 42tl, 43br, 45bl, 45bc, 46br, 47bc, 48tl, 49bl, 50cl, 50bl, 51bl, 51br, 52tl, 52b, 53br; Adam Ohringer :21l; Popperfoto 30bl, 38blk 45tr, 47bl; Powerstock/Zefa 48br; Science Museum/Science & Society Picture Library 36tl; Science Photo Library: 8tl, 10b, 12tl, 12br, 16tl, 18l, 18b, 21br, 38tl, 47br, 53tl; Karen L.Srivener: 31tl; Spectrum Colour Library: 16bl, 42br; Still Pictures: 7cr, 13bl, 13tr, 22tl; Trip: 5bl, 33br, 50br; Surveyor General's Department New South Wales, Australia: 5c, 29c.

Barite desert rose

CONTENTS

4 Introduction
6 Rock from rock
8 Making rocks
10 Wearing away
12 Sedimentary rocks
14 Turned to stone
16 Limestone
18 Fossils and fuels
20 Fiery mountains
22 Explosions!
24 Cooling underground
26 Changing rocks

28 Changed to marble
30 Building in stone
32 Stone tools
34 Minerals in rocks
36 Crystal clear
38 Coloring in
40 Decorative stones
42 The quartz family
44 Gems and jewelry
46 Modern tools
48 Precious metals
50 Metallic ores
52 Outer space
54 Index

Pyrite

This church in the Puy de Dôme in France is built on top of a volcanic plug. The plug formed when warm magma solidified inside a volcano. The rest of the volcano has long since worn away. This area in France is dotted with the remains of ancient volcanoes that are now extinct.

Churches and monasteries were often built on the highest point in an area.

INTRODUCTION

The surface of the Earth is astonishingly varied. It ranges from mountains to valleys, from deserts to deep seas. Much of the landscape is covered with vegetation, but this is merely a cover for its bare bones – the rocks that lie beneath it. The landscape is shaped by rocks that formed over billions of years and are still changing today. By studying the rocks, we can learn about the Earth's past and how it affects the present.

Rock ripples

ROCKY RIPPLES
Sand ripples left by a shallow sea on a beach millions of years ago are sometimes preserved as rock forms. Modern geologists study these rocks to learn about the landscape and the climate of the past.

RIPPLES IN THE SAND

A child is playing on rippled sand left by the receding tide. Scientists can learn about ripple patterns in rocks by studying ripples on our beaches today. They learn about wave action, tides, and depth of water by measuring the size of these ripples.

Ripples are formed by shallow water.

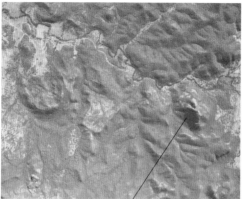

A dome-shaped hill rises above walls of rock.

GRANITE TORS

The rocks of Hay Tor on Dartmoor in England are made of hard granite. Millions of years of erosion have left them exposed on the surface of a high, barren landscape. They show that in the past this was an area of great upheaval.

VIEW FROM THE AIR

Aerial photography of rock formations shows the course and pattern of their creation. The Warrumbungles in Australia were once a huge center of volcanic activity. Today steep walls, needles, and domes of rock are all that remain of the range of volcanoes.

These rocks erode more slowly than the softer rock that once surrounded them.

BUILT IN LAYERS

Black biotite is a mineral with crystals that form in layers, rather like a pile of dinner plates. Atoms, the building blocks of a crystal, form three-dimensional structures that give a crystal its shape. Biotite crystals form strong layers that are weakly linked together. This means that layers can be easily split apart.

The layers split easily into thin, flexible, smooth, and shiny sheets of biotite.

ROCK FROM ROCK

Rocks and minerals are being made all the time, in a slow process that takes millions of years. Some are formed on the surface of the Earth and others deep beneath the ground. Rocks are made of minerals. They may be made of just one mineral or of a combination of different ones. Minerals show as different colors in the rock. Each mineral has its own structure and chemical makeup.

ROCK CYCLE

Rocks form, change shape, and wear away in a continuous cycle. Mountains form as a result of volcanic activity or under-ground movement, then gradually wear away. Fragments of rock travel down rivers into the sea, then build up as sediments that over time form layers of new rock.

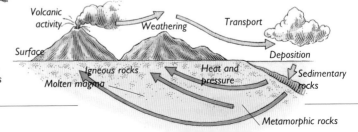

Volcanic activity. Weathering Transport

Surface Deposition

Igneous rocks Heat and pressure Sedimentary rocks

Molten magma

Metamorphic rocks

GRANITE CLOSE-UP

Granite is a rock formed deep below the surface of the Earth. The presence of different minerals in granite is shown by the various colors. The white and pink specks are feldspars, the specks of black are tourmaline, and the gray and clear fragments are quartz.

FELDSPAR

Feldspar is a common rock-forming mineral. The family of feldspar, includes orthoclase feldspar, which is used in the manufacture of porcelain and abrasive cleaners. Moonstones and clear yellow orthoclase are cut as gemstones. Blue microline is made into beads of polished amazonite.

White feldspar and gray quartz are the most numerous minerals in this granite.

RIVER TO ROCK

Pebbles, sand, and mud travel downstream to form layers of sediment in the sea. The weight of the overlying sediment makes the deepest layers of mud, sand, and pebbles form into rock under the pressure.

LANDSLIDE

Large landslides occur after heavy rainfall or earthquakes, especially in steep river valleys or where the rocks are still forming.

A landslide in a Swiss valley contains both fine pebbles and boulders.

7

MAKING ROCKS

The crust of the Earth is made up of giant interlocking plates called tectonic plates that carry the continents and oceans. The plates are always on the move. Over millions of years the continents change shape. Where plates move apart beneath the oceans, new seafloor is made as molten rock from within the Earth wells up. When plates collide, mountains are pushed up. Where plates overlap, part of the Earth's crust slips beneath the surface.

SAN ANDREAS FAULT LINE
Los Angeles and San Francisco in California are on the San Andreas fault system. A fault system can occur where two plates of the Earth's crust meet and scrape past each other, causing earthquakes.

FOLD MOUNTAINS
When two continental plates are pushed against each other they sometimes buckle upward to form a mountain chain. The Himalayas, the highest mountains on Earth, formed when two plates collided millions of years ago.

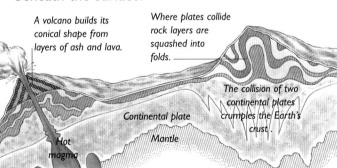

A volcano builds its conical shape from layers of ash and lava.

Where plates collide rock layers are squashed into folds.

The collision of two continental plates crumples the Earth's crust.

Continental plate

Mantle

Hot magma

8

MOUNTAINS AND VALLEYS

Les Gorges de Dalius in France formed when continental plates collided and pushed up rocks to form folded and faulted mountains, the Alps.

Water runs down the sides of mountains into a river, and washes away the valley floor.

VANISHING GROUND

The Earth's crust is constantly vanishing in places. When a thin oceanic plate pushes toward a thicker continental plate, it slides underneath the continental plate. Deep beneath the ground the rocks of the oceanic plate melt, causing earthquakes and volcanic eruptions.

NEW GROUND

Running down the center of the sea floor beneath the Atlantic Ocean is a long range of volcanoes called the Mid-Atlantic Ridge. This ridge formed along the margins of two tectonic plates. The volcanoes erupt lava that becomes new seafloor. As new sea floor is made Europe and America, carried on separate tectonic plates, move farther apart.

A trench is formed where an oceanic plate slips beneath a continental plate.

A ridge of volcanoes beneath the ocean where lava forms new oceanic crust. The oldest part of the oceanic crust is only about 200 million years old.

Ocean

Continental plate

Oceanic plate

Mid-Oceanic Ridge

Oceanic plate

This rock was once part of a glacier. It acted as a "scraper" against the rock walls and valley floor as the glacier moved forward.

WEARING AWAY

Weathering and erosion are constantly changing the surface of the Earth. Some changes are rapid, caused by landslides and floods. Others take place over thousands of years. Weathering can be chemical, such as the effects of acid rain, or physical, such as frost that causes rocks to split apart. The wearing away of rocks and the landscape by ice, wind, and water is called erosion.

RHÔNE GLACIER

These ice cliffs at the end of the Rhône Glacier in the Swiss Alps are moving slowly downhill. A glacier of ice and rocks has enough force to carve out the sides of a narrow V-shaped valley into a broad U-shape. As the ice melts it dumps piles of rock fragments called glacial moraine.

THE SPHINX

In about 2500 B.C., the Pharaoh Chephren built an amazing pyramid, temple, and sphinx at Giza, beside the River Nile. The sphinx was carved from nummulitic limestone quarried locally near Cairo. The face of the sphinx is believed to be a portrait of Chephren.

EGYPTIAN LIMESTONE

Nummulites are small sea animals. Over 40 million years ago their skeletons formed into rock, nummulitic limestone, beneath the sea. Over time the nummulitic limestone has been pushed up into the African landmass.

Fossil shells

For four and a half thousand years, the sphinx has been gradually eroded by grains of sand blown across the desert by the wind.

GRAND CANYON

The deepest gorge in the world has been cut out by the Colorado River in the U.S.A. Over thousands of years the river has carried millions of tons of rock downstream in the form of mud and sediment and created a canyon over 1 mile (1.6 km) deep.

11

SEDIMENTARY ROCKS

Mud and sand carried along by rivers, streams, and the sea gradually pile up in layers of sediment. As new layers build up over the centuries they press down on the older layers of sediment below, squashing them into a layered rock, called sedimentary rock. This type of rock is formed in wet marshes and peat bogs, but it is also found in some of the driest areas in the world, the deserts.

SANDSTONE

Sandstone is built up from layers of sand. Each layer is a different color. Over time the layers of rock can become distorted, or even be turned upside down. A close look at sandstone can reveal where the rock formed and whether it is the right way up.

Sand dunes are blown into different shapes by the wind.

SAND DUNES.

Deserts are covered by rocks and gravel, and some have large areas of sand dunes. When sand buried deep within a dune is compressed by the layers on top it becomes sandstone.

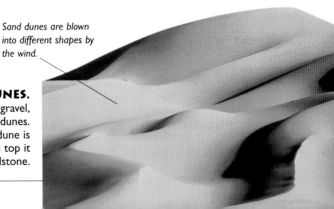

A DESERT ROSE

A rock made from small crystals of gypsum, a mineral formed in the desert where salt water has evaporated. Gypsum can form petallike crystals in the shape of a rose.

GRAVEL PIT

Gravel consists of small pebbles and jagged bits of rock that build up at the bottom of lakes and rivers, or on beaches. It is dug out of the ground at gravel pits and is usually washed to remove any sand or mud. Gravel is used in concrete and for surfacing roads.

These crystals are the first to form as salty water evaporates in arid areas.

MOUNT EVEREST

Mount Everest is in the Himalayas, a mountain range that formed when two continental plates collided. Among the rocks near the summit is limestone, formed on the ocean floor and pushed up by the collision.

SHALE

Shale is a dark, fragile rock made from clay or mud that settled in slow-moving rivers or mud flats. As layers of mud and clay are buried by new layers of sediment, the water in them is squeezed out and the lowest layers compact to form mudstones and claystones.

13

TURNED TO STONE

Unwary animals that become trapped in wet mud or tree resins are sometimes preserved as fossils within sedimentary rock as it forms. Usually only the hard shell or skeleton of an animal is preserved. Limestones are often made entirely of fragments of shell or other remains of sea animals. Desert sandstorms can bury animals, preserving their skeletons as fossils. Sometimes only an impression of the animal or its footprint remains.

CHALK CLIFF
The white cliffs of Dover in England are made of a fine-grained, white rock called chalk. It is formed from the skeletons of many millions of tiny sea animals that accumulated on the seabed in the late Cretaceous age. "Creta" is the Latin word for chalk.

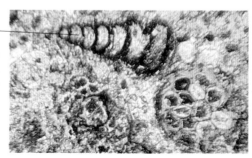

Radiolaria and foraminifera shells.

CLOSE-UP
The tiny shells of sea creatures preserved as chalk can be clearly seen under a microscope.

TREE RESIN

Resin protects a tree from disease. It is very sticky and oozes out of the bark when it is cut. If the resin becomes buried deep under the ground, over time, it turns to amber. Any insects that were caught in the resin are fossilized in the amber.

FOSSILS IN AMBER

Small animals caught in amber usually rot from the inside out, leaving only their shell or skeleton behind. It is extremely difficult to extract genetic material from their remains, and not enough genetic material can be found to create a dinosaur for a real "Jurassic Park.." The remarkable feature of insect fossils in amber is the perfect preservation of their hard, transparent wings.

STONE CRAB

This fossil crab looks just like a crab you could find today. Studying it and the rock around it can tell scientists how and where the crab lived and about the climate at the time.

The crab's eyes

This lifelike fly is a fossil. Amber containing insects can be used in jewelry.

15

LIMESTONE

Limestone is made mainly of calcium carbonate. It forms on the seabed, and is built up in layers usually from the skeletons of tiny sea creatures. Limestone may be forced upward by underground movement or dissolved by acids in rainwater. It is found high up on mountains that have been pushed up from the seafloor. It is also found under-ground in caves, as stalactites and stalagmites.

LIMESTONE PAVEMENT
The deep crevices in limestone pavement are caused by rainwater settling in cracks and dissolving the limestone. Beneath limestone pavements there may be a maze of caves.

Limestone hills have very steep sides carved out by rainwater running down them.

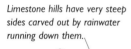

KNOBBY HILLS
Steep-sided limestone hills and gorges are known as karst scenery, such as the Guilan Hills in China. The knobby hills have been created by rainwater eroding the limestone.

LIMESTONE POOLS
At the hot springs in Pamukkale in Turkey, calcium carbonate deposited by the water has formed spectacular limestone pools and terraces.

LIMESTONE CAVE

Spectacular caves often form beneath limestone. Underground streams erode the rock into a system of caves. Lime (calcium carbonate), dissolves from the dripping rainwater, creating fantastic finger-like stalactites on the ceiling and stalagmites on the floor of the cave.

Knobby branches form as water drips from the cave ceiling.

STALAGMITE

As rainwater drops fall from the roof of the cave and land on the floor, a stalagmite may form. The stalagmite gradually builds up from the floor beneath a stalactite. If the two meet a column forms. It may take several thousand years for a stalagmite to grow one inch (25 mm).

Surface crystals glitter in the light.

STALACTITE

An icicle-shaped stalactite that hangs from the roof of a cave is formed by a solution of dissolved limestone dripping from above. As the drops dry, calcium carbonate is left and grows into a stalactite. The biggest stalactite in the world is more than 20 ft (6.2 m) long.

FOSSILS AND FUELS

DROP OF OIL
Oil is formed over millions of years from the bodies of plankton and tiny animals that lived in swamps and shallow seas. Buried under layers of sedimentary rock, deep underground, their remains were slowly converted to petroleum or crude oil.

Oil, coal, and natural gas were once living organisms. Plants and animals living in swamps, forests, and shallow seas during the Carboniferous period, about 300 million years ago, were sometimes buried before they rotted. Their remains were sandwiched between layers of rock-forming material, and, compacted by the weight above, they became fuel. The greater the pressure and heat on the fuel as it develops, the more pure carbon it contains and the more heat it generates when burned.

Oil is a convenient fuel to use because it is a liquid. It can be sent along pipes and switched on and off.

In Ireland, peat is dug out of the ground. It has been used as fuel for many generations.

PEAT BOG
Peat is compacted plant remains, the first stage in the geological process that forms coal. Plants are buried, and the water squashed out of them by the layers of sediment on top. Roots and seeds are clearly visible in peat.

18

FOSSIL FERN

A single fern leaf was trapped between layers of sediment or mud, and has been preserved in fine detail. When the cellulose in the leaf was replaced by minerals, it was transformed into a fossil over 300 million years ago.

COAL OR WOOD?

Coal was often part of a tree and may still look like wood. Buried under layers of sediment before it could decay, it retains its original shape but undergoes a chemical change to become coal.

PETRIFIED WOOD

Petrified means "turned to stone." Mineral quartz replaces the structures of the living wood. The tree is still recognizable in stone.

The details on this fossilized fern show that it was similar to many ferns that exist today.

Tree bark and growth rings made of stone.

FIERY MOUNTAINS

Volcanoes erupt when hot molten rock from deep within the Earth forces its way to the surface. The ground splits and the partially molten rock, called magma, wells up or erupts. Once magma is erupted, it is called lava. Some volcanoes are fairly predictable. They erupt and produce fast-flowing rivers of runny basalt lava. These volcanoes are often in areas where the tectonic plates are moving apart, and new oceanic crust is forming.

RIVERS OF LAVA

The volcanoes in Hawaii send out runny lava that spreads quickly, burning and scorching vast areas of land. These volcanoes usually erupt quietly, and the lava cools quickly to form fine-grained basalt rock. Iceland has many volcanoes that erupt basalt.

This runny lava is known in Hawaii as pahoehoe lava. It has a glassy surface and a ropelike structure.

DEVASTATION ERUPTS

Many people live beside volcanoes because the soil is fertile. When the volcano erupts, people are forced to flee, as they did from the island of Montserrat in 1997.

HARD BUBBLE

Dense black basalt lava often cools so quickly that bubbles of gas are trapped inside it. Balls of fragile, needle-sharp crystals of zeolite minerals form from the bubbles of gas.

A rock bubble full of prickly crystal balls

POWER STATION

In New Zealand some power stations are run on energy provided by underground volcanic activity, which they convert to electricity.

This lava has a smooth, glassy surface because it cooled so quickly there was no time for crystals to form.

EXPLOSIONS!

The most dangerous volcanoes are those that erupt violently, without much warning. Thick, sticky lava can block a volcano's vents, or openings, and trap gas so that the pressure inside builds up. When the volcano erupts there is an enormous explosion. The top of the volcano may be completely blown off. Explosive volcanoes throw out tons of lethal rocks and ashes, which can totally destroy nearby towns and villages.

Mount Etna

ERUPTIONS

Volcanoes such as Mount Etna in Sicily are active. This means that they are erupting regularly. Stromboli in Italy erupts several times a day. Other volcanoes are dormant ("sleeping"), but volcanic activity continues beneath the surface and they will probably erupt again.

Bone from victim of Mount Vesuvius

VICTIM'S BONE

The eruption of Mount Vesuvius in Italy in A.D. 79 buried nearby towns in ash and mud, but it was the burning gases that killed most people. A red-hot cloud of ash flowed down the mountain at speeds over 100 mph (160 kph).

WELDED NAILS

This lump of iron is a pile of nails melted at temperatures over 1,300°F (600°C), by the violent eruption of the volcano Mont Pelée on the island of Martinique in May 1902. A cloud of scorching ash, mud, and steam, carrying boulders and molten rock, poured out of the volcano in a destructive tide.

VOLCANIC ASH

Magnified, volcanic ash shows the channels formed by escaping gas. Mount St. Helens erupted in 1980, sending ash over an area of 580 square miles (1,500 sq km), and blocking out the sun.

INSIDE A VOLCANO

The cone shape of a volcano is built up by layers of ash and lava deposited around a central vent. Magma can be stored in chambers below the vent and may escape from side vents.

The soft and spongelike appearance of pumice disguises its hard, scratchy, and abrasive surface.

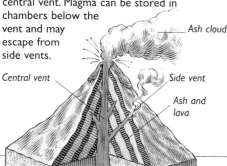

Central vent

Ash cloud

Side vent

Ash and lava

SCRUBBING STONE

Pumice is a light rock full of bubblelike holes. It is formed when foaming lava cools quickly enough for gases to become trapped inside. These gases make pumice light enough to float on water.

x

23

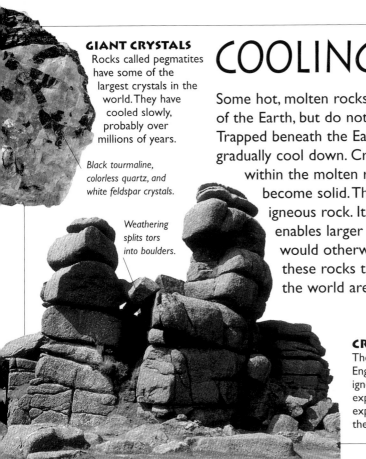

GIANT CRYSTALS

Rocks called pegmatites have some of the largest crystals in the world. They have cooled slowly, probably over millions of years.

Black tourmaline, colorless quartz, and white feldspar crystals.

Weathering splits tors into boulders.

COOLING DOWN

Some hot, molten rocks rise toward the surface of the Earth, but do not erupt from volcanoes. Trapped beneath the Earth's surface, they gradually cool down. Crystals form in bubbles within the molten rocks as they cool and become solid. This type of rock is called igneous rock. Its slow cooling process enables larger crystals to grow than would otherwise be possible. It is in these rocks that the largest crystals in the world are forming today.

CRACKING STONES

The granite tors of Dartmoor in England are isolated outcrops of igneous rock that have been exposed by erosion. The granite expands slightly and cracks when there is no longer any rock above it.

VOLCANIC PIPE

Magma that solidifies in the neck of a volcano forms a shape known as a pipe. Erosion exposes this hard core of the volcano. Over millions of years weather can reduce it to a sharp pinnacle of rock.

ROCK BALL

Geodes (rock balls) are bubbles of liquid or gas that have formed in cooling magma. The hard quartz that forms inside contains small amounts of iron that make it purple.

Amethyst crystals grow slowly inward, protected by the geode.

DIAMONDS

Diamonds are formed 50 miles (80 km) or more beneath the surface of the ground at enormous pressures and temperatures. The igneous rock kimberlite was once molten rock that solidified deep underground. It contains diamonds.

Diamond

EX-VOLCANO

Sugar Loaf Mountain overlooks Rio de Janeiro in Brazil and is all that remains of a plug of magma that hardened into a volcanic cone. The erosion of softer rocks capping the mountain has revealed a dome of igneous rock.

CHANGING ROCKS

High temperatures and pressures deep beneath the ground can make rocks change. Soft mudstone becomes harder and its layers are contorted as they are squashed and squeezed out of shape. These rocks have metamorphosed – changed their shape or form. Higher temperatures and pressures can even change the minerals within the rocks. These minerals are a clue to the temperatures and pressures involved.

GLORIOUS MUD
The mud of today may become mudstone in the future. As mud is buried, the weight of overlying sediments and the increased heat underground compacts it. Water is driven out and the mud becomes mudstone.

TURNING TO SHALE
Mudstone and clays become shales when pressure and increased temperature change the structure of the rock. Shale can be split along the layers of the rock, giving it an uneven surface. Shale often contains fossils.

SHALE TO SLATE
Shale becomes slate when the temperature and pressure underground are increased. It is often used to make roof tiles.

SLATE TO SCHIST

The temperatures needed to form schist from slate are at least 932°F (500°C), higher than those that form slate. Schist has a shiny, sparkling appearance, with wavy folds.

The Alps are a long chain of mountains

A SLICE OF SCHIST

Under a microscope a thin slice of schist shows different colored minerals in thin, parallel layers.

Mountain peaks and valleys are formed when rock layers are folded under pressure.

THE ALPS

These mountains were formed as a result of the collision of tectonic plates. The increased temperatures and pressures caused some of the rocks to be changed into metamorphic rocks.

This gneiss from Amitsoq Bay, Greenland, is about 3,800 million years old.

GNEISS ENDING

At high temperatures and pressures, igneous and sedimentary rocks may be transformed to gneiss. Gneiss has a coarser grain than schist and is recognizable because its minerals usually separate into bands that fold under pressure.

CHANGED TO MARBLE

Marble is metamorphosed limestone. When limestone is exposed to high temperatures and great pressure deep beneath the ground the rock becomes harder and more compressed. New crystals of calcite also grow within it, changing the limestone into marble. Marble varies enormously in color, texture, and pattern. It can be cut and polished which has made it a popular stone to use in buildings and for carving into statues.

UNCUT MARBLE
The texture and pattern that make polished marble such a prized decorative stone is not as clear in a rough piece of marble.

Bianco venato marble comes from the famous Carrara quarry in Italy. It was used by the great sculptors of the Renaissance.

Cipollino marble from Greece

Polished granite is often used in place of marble.

CUT AND POLISHED
Large saws are used to cut marble into blocks and then slabs. The slabs are polished and used to decorate buildings. Temples built of marble by the Greeks 2,500 years ago are deteriorating as acid rain dissolves the stone, causing permanent damage to the surface of the marble.

The layers of limestone in this hill have been pushed up and folded into place through tremendous underground pressure.

FOSSILS IN LIMESTONE

Fossils can often be seen in polished slabs of limestone. Erne limestone from Ireland has the fossils of tiny sea creatures and plants, including the stems of sea lilies, that lived millions of years ago.

LIMESTONE QUARRY

Limestone that formed from sediment on the seabed, over millions of years, has become part of the Australian landmass. The hilltop has been dug to provide limestone for building.

The minute fossil stem of a sea lily.

Sculptors work on rough marble. Polishing completes the statue.

MICHELANGELO'S SLAVE

This statue was carved from white Carrara marble, which is easily worked. It does not contain obvious fossils or cracks. The quarries of Carrara in Italy were famous during the Renaissance. They are still in use today.

BUILDING IN STONE

Glazed tiles were first used in Mesopotamia, an area that lacked suitable stone for carving. Thousands of years later in Jerusalem, the same type of tile was used to decorate the Dome of the Rock, a mosque, built in 687 A.D. Below the golden dome, blue tiles represent heaven. Tiles colored green and yellow represent earth.

Many buildings, such as the pyramids in Egypt, have survived for thousands of years because they were built of stone. Ancient craftsmen were able to cut stone very accurately. Today, modern building materials are constructed from the same ingredients as stone. They are precast into reinforced concrete blocks, bricks, and glass. Thin slabs of natural stone facing are also often used to decorate buildings, both inside and out.

Glazed tiles are painted with a clay-wash and baked. The glaze forms a hard, shiny surface on the tile.

ROMAN MOSAIC

The Romans made different colored stone, glass, and other materials into small cubes that they called "tesserae." These were then arranged into pictures and set in cement to make a colorful mosaic. Figures were often outlined with cubes of black marble or basalt.

CEMENT

The crystal structure of cement can be seen under a microscope. Cement powder is made by mixing crushed limestone and clay. Mixed with sand and water, it is called mortar and used for building with bricks.

BRICKS AND MORTAR

Many buildings are made of bricks held together by cement, which acts like glue and hardens as it dries. Bricks are made from clay and earth. They are pressed into blocks and baked at a very high temperature until hard.

Bricks were first used for building in the ancient world.

TWO-TONE STONE

Labradorite, a decorative building stone, is a type of feldspar. It comes from Labrador in Canada. When it is polished, it appears to change colour from gray to blue, as light moves over the surface.

POLISHED STONE

The range of colors and patterns in marble make it a useful decorative stone. The Chapel of the Princes in Florence has walls and floors of polished marble. It contains the marble tombs of some of the Medici family, who built it.

STONE TOOLS

Stones have been made into tools for over two million years. All sorts of fine-grained rocks were used because they are easy to chip (nap) into shape. Choppers, hammers, and scrapers were used to kill and skin animals, to prepare food, and to build shelters. Wooden handles were carved with stone blades. The first farmers used stone knives to harvest wheat, and two flat stones to grind the wheat to flour.

When obsidian breaks it leaves a curved shape with razor-sharp edges.

BLACK GLASS

Obsidian is a glassy black stone that forms when volcanic lava cools rapidly. Obsidian was declared sacred by the ancient Maya of Central America, who believed it formed when lightning struck the ground. They carved portraits of their gods on obsidian flake-daggers.

FLINT ARROWHEAD

Flint is a rock formed from fine-grained silica. When struck at an angle by a hammer-stone, a flake breaks off, leaving a razor-sharp edge. Further chipping produces the desired shape.

The wooden arrow shaft which held this arrowhead has rotted away.

CATAPULT

A catapult is a simple machine for throwing rocks. The Romans built huge catapults to hurl rocks over the walls of their enemies. Catapults were replaced when cannons were able to send balls of stone or iron greater distances.

STONE HAND AX

Early man used stone axes for smashing open bones. Inside bones there is a protein-rich store of soft, edible bone marrow. Axes were also used to chop up plants to eat. A stone ax can be made in minutes. The blade does not remain sharp once the ax has been used,so it is discarded and a new ax is made.

SLAVE KILLER

The stone club was used in religious ceremonies by the Kwakiutl people from the Northwest coast of America. Traces of red powder (ochre) on the stone may have been applied to look like blood. The club may have been occasionally used to kill slaves.

Stone club

GRINDING STONE

A Berber woman is grinding wheat into flour using grinding stones. Small pieces of grit from the stones mix with the flour and wear down the teeth of people who eat it.

33

MINERALS IN ROCKS

Tourmaline crystals are used as gemstones.

Rocks are made up of minerals. Each mineral has its own chemistry, which is different from that of every other mineral. There are about 3,500 minerals, and more are being discovered every year. Each mineral is identified by a set of characteristics, or properties. These include structure, hardness, color, and the shape of its crystals. Most rocks are made of more than one mineral.

TOURMALINE CRYSTAL

Tourmaline exists in almost every color. The colors are due partly to its complex chemical makeup. Tourmaline is found in granite, a rock formed from the minerals quartz and feldspar.

MOHS' SCALE OF HARDNESS

The Austrian scientist Friedrich Mohs graded 10 minerals according to their hardness. Each mineral on the scale can be scratched by the minerals above it, but not by those below it. The Mohs scale ranges from talc, the softest mineral, to diamond, the hardest one. The scale does not increase in equal steps. The difference between corundum (ruby) and diamond is greater than that between talc and corundum.

Talc → Gypsum → Calcite → Fluorite → Apatite → Orthoclase

WULFENITE

Wulfenite is bright yellow and forms as stacks of fragile plate-like crystals. It is a lead mineral and is used in the manufacture of steel to increase its hardness.

The layers of crystal stack up into flat-topped pyramids.

HEMATITE

Hematite can form as thin platelike crystals or as large rounded boulders. Hematite contains the mineral iron. Most reddish-colored rocks contain iron. Powdered hematite is used as a polish for jewelry.

Each crystal has 18 facets or faces.

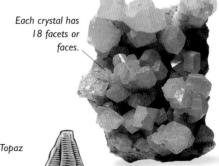

SULPHUR

Sulphur crystallizes as bright yellow crystals, and is one of the few minerals that are always the same color. Clusters of sulphur crystals are often found around hot springs and the vents of volcanoes.

Quartz → *Topaz* → *Corundum* → *Diamond*

CRYSTAL CLEAR

Most minerals are made of crystals. Crystals grow in a fantastic variety of geometric shapes. They can be long and spiky, rounded, or shaped like cubes. Some have regular symmetrical features and smooth, flat surfaces, called faces. How crystals develop depends on their atomic structure and the conditions in which they grow. Most gemstones are natural crystals chosen for their beauty and rarity.

Headphones used for listening.

CRYSTAL RADIO

Quartz crystals were used in radio sets because they vibrate at a regular rate in response to electricity. Quartz is a common mineral, and quartz crystals can be found all around the world. Nowadays, however, it is also produced artificially to the required size.

AMETHYST

Groups of amethyst crystals form in cavities in magma. In a large cavity the clusters can grow as large as 10 ft (3 m) across. Amethyst is a transparent purple variety of quartz. Its crystals form six-sided prisms with one pointed end.

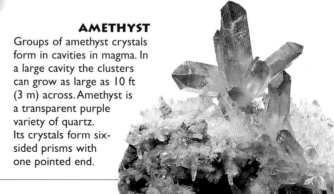

FOOL'S GOLD
Pyrite is often called fool's gold. Its regular, cube-shaped crystals are so shiny that they look as if they have been cut and polished, but they are completely natural and form like this within rocks. Pyrite is actually paler in color than yellow gold. Unlike real gold, it is very hard.

These crystals are the same shape even though they are not always the same size.

ZIRCON
Zircon crystals have pyramid-shaped ends. They can be heated to change their color to blue, golden-brown or colorless stones. They can be cut and polished as gemstones.

Zircon

Fluorite crystal

FLUORESCENT CRYSTAL
Like pyrite, fluorite has cube-shaped crystals. Fluorite belongs to a group of minerals that appear to change color under ultraviolet light. They become "fluorescent" and glow with a different color as the light interacts with atoms within the crystals.

Topaz crystal

TOPAZ
Topaz has a greasy-feeling surface. Its crystals are diamond-shaped in cross-section. The straight grooves are not scratches but growth lines that formed as the topaz crystal grew.

COLORING IN

The natural colors of powdered rocks and minerals have been used to make colors called pigments for paints and dyes since prehistoric times. Early man mixed water with ochre, a dry clay powder, to paint on the walls of caves. Over the centuries brighter colors were found. Today, many colors are produced synthetically but pigments are still made by crushing rocks and minerals into powder.

Figures in procession

CAVE PAINTING
The figures in the Kolo cave painting from Kenya in Africa were painted using an ocher mixture. Archaeologists estimate the cave painting to be at least 25,000 years old.

"Mad...
and ...
by Gi...
Bellin...

POISONOUS POWDER
Arsenic is a poisonous mineral. Roman ladies used powdered arsenic to whiten their skin. The poison can be absorbed by the skin. It slowly builds up in the body and eventually causes paralysis and death.

Arsenic

FOOTBALL COLORS
Some football fans paint their faces with their team's colors as a symbol of support. Some paints contain natural mineral pigments.

POWDERY CRYSTALS

Rough crystals of azurite can be completely reduced to powder and used as pigment. Azurite makes the oil paint known as cerulean or Armenian blue. Azurite is a hard ornamental stone. It is often found with the decorative green stone malachite.

Hard blue azurite crystals

PRECIOUS BLUE

In medieval times a rock called lapis lazuli was crushed to make the precious blue paint pigment ultramarine. It was used particularly for the Madonna's clothing in medieval paintings.

DECORATIVE STONE

Turquoise was valued for its sky blue color by early civilizations, such as the Persians and Aztecs, who used it for jewelry thousands of years ago. Early North American Indians also prized, turquoise which they found in the southwestern United States.

Native North American ornament

BLUE VEINS

The size of a piece of turquoise is determined by the size of the turquoise veins found within rock. Turquoise gets its blue color from copper.

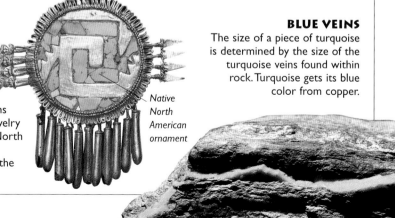

DECORATIVE STONES

Jeweled headdress from Ur.

The colors and textures of many rocks make them ideal for carving into decorative pieces. Rocks have been used to make jewelry, bowls, masks, and amulets or lucky charms. Some rocks have special qualities; they sparkle or shine when held up to the light and when they are polished. Stones have been used to make beads and other jewelry for nearly 7,000 years. Some ancient people believed that certain rocks possessed magical powers.

A QUEEN'S JEWELS

Fine jewels were found in the grave of an ancient Sumerian queen at Ur in Iraq. They were made in about 2,500 B.C. from gold, lapis lazuli, and carnelian.

JADEITE MASK

Jadeite is the most valuable of the two jades, jadeite and nephrite. The early civilizations of South America used jadeite to make masks and other pieces of religious significance, as well as jewelry.

Nephrite "tiki"

BIG EYES
For hundreds of years, nephrite jade boulders found in the rivers of South Island, New Zealand, have been carved into small figures or "tikis." A big-eyed "tiki" represents a sacred Maori figure and would have been worn around someone's neck.

A stripe of reflective quartz

MOVING IN THE LIGHT
"Tiger's-eye" forms when the long, silky fibers of crocidolite (asbestos) are replaced by quartz. Polishing the stone allows light to reflect from the quartz structure within the stone. When the stone is moved the line or "tiger's eye" appears to shift across its surface.

Sacred scarab beetle

The bright sparkles in sunstone are caused by light reflecting on tiny flakes of hematite within the stone.

CHINESE HAIRPIN
During the Ming dynasty in China, hairpins were some-times made from sunstone, a type of feldspar.

BLUE BEETLE
This decorative scarab, or beetle, was carved out of lapis lazuli by the ancient Egyptians. The best lapis lazuli comes from Afghanistan, far from Egypt. In the past, decorative stones were carried hundreds of miles from their source along trade routes.

QUARTZ FAMILY

Quartz is one of the most common minerals, and it is also one of the most varied. Its forms include white quartz sand on the beach, banded agates, and the crystal treasure troves found inside hollow geodes. Although quartz occurs in an amazing array of colors and shapes, all quartz has the same chemical structure: it is silicon dioxide – a simple combination of silicon and oxygen.

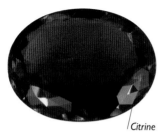

Citrine

CITRINE

Citrine is quartz and can be cut to show off its color and sparkle. The color varies from golden yellow to deep brown. Only the clearest citrine is used as gemstones. The darkest varieties imitate the more valuable gemstone topaz.

MULTICOLORED CRYSTALS

Large, smoky, grayish-brown quartz is found in the Cairngorm Mountains in Scotland and in Brazil. The largest crystal found in Brazil weighs 650 lb (300 kg).

Smoky quartz

WHITE SAND

The sand grains on some beaches are mainly made of quartz, which has been washed down from mountains to the sea by rivers and streams. With every tide, the sand grains are rolled back and forth, rounding their edges a little more.

GHOST CRYSTAL

While this quartz crystal was growing, a brief change in conditions led to it being coated by another mineral. When the colorless quartz continued to grow, it trapped a mineral outline of its smaller, earlier self like a "ghost."

Quartz crystals are usually six-sided, with one pointed end.

The "ghost" crystal, is visible only because it is thinly coated with another mineral.

TREASURE BALL

Thunder eggs or potato stones are the names for geodes, the balls of rock that form around gas bubbles in volcanic lava and magma as they cool. On the inside of a geode quartz crystals grow towards the center.

QUARTZ CRYSTALS

A coating of a mineral called limonite covers these quartz crystals. Under the limonite there is clear, colorless rock crystal. The pointed end is a six-sided pyramid. Other well-known varieties of quartz are agate, amethyst, chalcedony, jasper, and rock crystal.

Banded agate

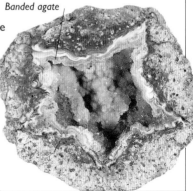

GEMS AND JEWELRY

People have been attracted to gemstones since the earliest times. Gemstones are natural minerals. They are exceptional because they are beautiful and rare. The rarer a gemstone, the more valuable it is. Gemstones have to be durable, to stand up to everyday use as jewelry. Diamonds, rubies, emeralds, and sapphires are all gemstones. Held up to the light, they sparkle and their colors glow.

In Borneo a man looks for diamonds amidst the sediment left in his pan.

RIVER DIAMONDS
In Indonesia, Thailand, and Sri Lanka diamonds are found in rivers. Sediment piles up where the water slows down round bends. Gem seekers "pan" through the sediment. They wash away the mud and lighter material, and look for gem stones in the heavier pebbles at the bottom of the pan.

DIAMOND MINE
The first diamonds discovered within rock were found in South Africa just over 100 years ago. Diamonds have been mined there ever since.

This is an aerial view into the open pit of the modern Finsch diamond mine in South Africa, owned by De Beers.

PRECIOUS STONES

Only about 50 varieties of mineral are commonly used as gemstones. They have three qualities in common: their beauty, durability and rarity. Cutting and polishing emphasizes these qualities.

DIAMOND TIARAS

Diamonds, the best-known gemstones, have been used in all sorts of jewelry, from crowns to engagement rings.

A long boule (stick) of ruby is made first. It is cut into gemstones later.

RUBY COPY

Rubies have a simple chemistry that scientists have been able to copy in the laboratory since the beginning of the 20th century. Synthetic rubies are used in lasers, watches, and also in jewelry.

Diamond   *Emerald*

Sapphire   *Ruby*

CUT STONES

The angles of the flat sides, or facets, of a gemstone are worked out mathematically to let as much light as possible into the front of the stone (the largest facet). The light is then reflected back out of the stone, making it sparkle.

MODERN TOOLS

As our technology advances, our need to use minerals increases. Inside every computer there is a silicon chip. Diamonds are used to make sharp scalpels and drills for surgery. Rubies are employed in lasers. These minerals, and many others used by industry, are usually made in a laboratory. They have the same chemical, physical, and optical properties as the natural minerals they copy.

INDUSTRIAL DIAMONDS

Many diamonds are not good enough to be cut as gems for jewelry. Some are still useful, however, and are called industrial diamonds. These diamonds can also be made in a laboratory. These synthetic diamonds are just as hard as natural diamonds.

DIAMOND SCALPEL

Scientists can produce films of diamond that can can be sprayed onto scalpel blades in thin layers. The diamonds provide an incredibly sharp, fine cutting edge for use in delicate operations on the eye.

Diamond coated blade

QUARTZ WATCH

Natural quartz vibrates at a steady rate in reaction to an electrical charge. Synthetic quartz made in a laboratory has none of the imperfections of some natural quartz. It is used in watches to keep time accurately.

DIAMOND DRILL

The hardest natural substance is diamond. It can scratch or cut any other material. This tiny drill head is studded with diamond chippings.

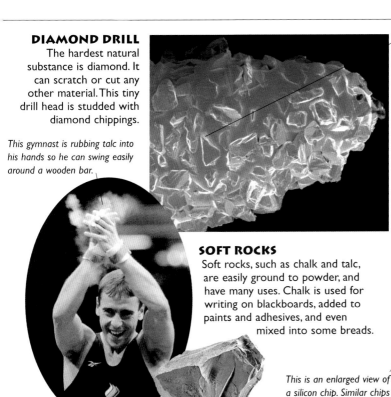

This gymnast is rubbing talc into his hands so he can swing easily around a wooden bar.

Sharply angled diamond chips cover a drill head. As the drill rotates, the diamonds grind into any surface.

CRYSTAL CHIP

A silicon chip is made of microscopic electrical components mounted on a piece of synthetic silicon crystal. Scientists are working to produce smaller silicon chips for more specialized uses, especially in medicine.

SOFT ROCKS

Soft rocks, such as chalk and talc, are easily ground to powder, and have many uses. Chalk is used for writing on blackboards, added to paints and adhesives, and even mixed into some breads.

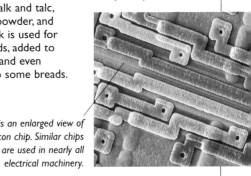

This is an enlarged view of a silicon chip. Similar chips are used in nearly all electrical machinery.

Platinum nugget

PRECIOUS METALS

The most precious metals are platinum, gold, and silver. Small grains or nuggets of gold can be found in river sediments. Such "finds" inspired the gold rushes of the 19th century, when thousands of gold-seekers converged at the site of a "find". Gold, platinum, and silver are usually extracted from metal-bearing rock deposits, which must be crushed before the metal can be extracted.

PRECIOUS PLATINUM

Platinum is the most valuable of the precious metals and is also the rarest. It occurs as minute grains within rocks or, rarely, as nuggets. Unlike silver, the surface of platinum does not tarnish or darken when exposed to the air.

GOLD MINE

Modern mining methods make use of large cutting and crushing machines. After mining the rock may be treated with chemicals or heated, to recover the gold. South Africa produces more gold than any other country in the world.

A productive gold mine in northeastern Canada

CHUNK OF GOLD

The largest gold nugget ever found weighed 159 lb (70.92 kg). In 1848 gold was found in California by a carpenter. This led to the first rush of diggers seeking gold. In 1851, there was a gold rush to Australia. and to South Africa in 1886.

SILVER BRANCHES

Silver found in a pure form in the ground is called native silver. Its structure is called dendritic, meaning branch-like. Platinum and gold are also found in these delicate shapes, although usually they are found combined with other metals.

Delicate branches of silver

GOLD PANNING

When people look for gold nuggets in river sediment they use a metal pan to scoop up gravel and water. When the pan is swirled around, the water and lighter material are splashed out, while the heavier gold collects in the pan. The grains of gold are usually small, so the rewards of panning for gold are few.

Mercury is the only metal that is liquid at room temperature. When it is split, it forms drops or balls. These balls join together again on contact. Mercury is used to register temperature in thermometers.

METALLIC ORES

Ore is the name given to rock that contains enough of a particular metal to make mining it worthwhile. Once mined, the rock has to be processed to extract the metal. This can be done by crushing the rock mechanically or breaking it down using acids. Once the ore is extracted, it is refined and smelted to produce metal. It can then be cast into shape. The use of metals such as bronze and iron identify stages of progress in civilization.

Ball of mercury

Chromite

BRIGHT AND SHINY

Chromite is the the ore of chromium. Chromium does not rust and has an attractive shiny surface. It is used to manufacture stainless steel, and in metallic paints. It is also used as plating to cover other metals. Handles, taps, and plugs can be chrome-plated.

COG WHEEL ORE

The crystals of cog wheel ore are rare. They resemble small mechanical cog wheels similar to the wheels used to keep time in wind-up watches. Cog wheel ore contains the mineral chromite, although it is difficult to extract from crystals.

Crystals of galena

Colorless crystals of quartz

TIN PLATES

Cassiterite is a tin ore, sometimes called "tinstone." Tin melts easily, which makes it useful for solder and tinplate. Tinplate is a sheet of steel coated with a thin layer of tin that stops it from rusting. Tin is mixed with lead to make pewter, and copper to make bronze.

Flat, platelike crystals of cassiterite

GALENA

Crystals of galena form as near-perfect cubes underground, and look as though they have been cut and polished. Galena is the main ore of lead, an important metal used to make lead sheeting. Galena is also a major source of silver and may contain up to 1%. The ore is usually mined for lead with silver as a by-product.

51

OUTER SPACE

Rocks from space that land on Earth are called meteorites. They are fragments of asteroids, rocks that orbit the sun or the other planets. Thousands of meteorites fall every year but few of them are found. They are valuable clues to the history of the Solar System and how it may have formed. Rocks brought back from space missions by astronauts have helped scientists to trace the history of the Moon.

A fusion of rock and metal   Meteorite

METEORITE
The most common meteorites are made of rock. Others are partly or entirely made of iron. Meteorites can range in size from dust particles to objects many (miles) kilometres in diameter. Large meteorites that crash into Earth make huge craters.

METEORITE FROM MARS
Eight meteorites found in Antarctica are thought to have come from Mars. They contain tiny shapes, which might be fossils of Martian bacteria that lived millions of years ago. Other meteorites found in Antarctica are similar in structure to rocks found on the Moon.

CRATER
A crater in Arizona was made by a large meteorite that hit Earth millions of years ago. The force of its impact made it smash into small fragments, thousands of which have been found nearby.

Craters filled with lava are called "mares" or seas. They are visible from the Earth.

MOON CRATER
The Moon is covered in circular craters, the result of intense bombardment by meteorites over billions of years. Because there is no rain on the Moon, there is almost no erosion, so its surface has hardly changed in over 400 million years.

MOON ROCK
Some rocks brought back to Earth by astronauts on the Apollo 15 mission are volcanic rocks called basalt. They are probably more than 3,000 million years old.

MEN ON THE MOON
The first men to land on the Moon were Neil Armstrong and Buzz Aldrin in 1969. They collected 48 lb (22 kg) of rocks for scientists on Earth to study. Their footprints will probably remain for over 100 million years on the Moon.

53

INDEX

A

acid rain, 10, 28
Afghanistan, 41
agate, 42, 43
Aldrin, Buzz, 53
Alps, 9, 10, 27
amazonite, 7
amber, 15
amethyst, 25, 36, 43
animals, fossils, 14-15
Antarctica, 52
apatite, 34
Armenian blue, 39
Armstrong, Neil, 53
arrowheads, 32

Fossil Crab

arsenic, 38
asbestos, 41
ash, volcanic, 22, 23
asteroids, 52
atoms, crystals, 6, 36
Australia, 5, 29, 49
axes, stone, 33
Aztecs, 39
azurite, 39

B

Bainco venato marble, 28
basalt, 30, 53
basalt lava, 20, 21

Berbers, 33
biotite, 6
Borneo, 44
Brazil, 42
bricks, 31
bronze, 50, 51
building materials, 30-1

C

Cairngorm Mountains,
    42
calcite, 28, 34
calcium carbonate, 16,
    17
California, 8, 49
carbon, 18
Carboniferous period,
    18
carnelian, 40
Carrara marble, 29
carvings, 40-1
cassiterite, 51
catapults, 33

cave paintings, 38
caves, limestone, 16-17
cement, 31
Central America, 32
cerulean blue, 39
chalk, 14, 47
Chephren, Pharaoh, 11
China, 41
chromite, 50, 51
chromium, 50
citrine, 43
clay, bricks, 31
claystones, 13
clubs, stone, 33
coal, 18, 19
Colorado River, 11
colors, pigments, 38-9
continental plates, 8-9,
    13, 27
copper, 39, 51
corundum, 34, 35
crabs, fossil, 15
craters, meteorite, 52,
    53

crust, Earth's, 8-9
crystals, 34-7
  igneous rock, 24
  quartz, 42-3
  shapes, 6

D

Dartmoor, 5, 24
De Beers, 44
desert rose, 13
deserts, 12, 14
diamonds:
  formation, 25
  hardness, 34, 35
  industrial uses, 46, 47
  jewelry, 44, 45
  mining, 44
Dome of the Rock,
  Jerusalem, 30
dormant, volcano, 22
Dover, 14
dunes, sand, 12

E

Egypt, Ancient, 41
emeralds, 44, 45
erosion, 10-11, 24-5, 53
eruptions, volcanoes, 9,
  20, 22-3
Etna, Mount, 22
Everest, Mount, 13

F

fault systems, 8
feldspar, 7
  labradorite, 31
  sunstone, 41
ferns, fossil, 19
flint, 32
Florence, 31
fluorite, 34, 37
fold mountains, 8
fool's gold, 37
fossils, 14-15, 29
France, 4, 9
fuels, fossil, 18-19

G

galena, 51
gas, natural, 18
gemstones, 36-7, 44-
  5
geodes, 25, 42, 43
Giza, 11
glaciers, 10
gneiss, 27
gold, 40, 48, 49
Gorges de
  Dalius, 9
Grand Canyon, 11
granite:
  minerals, 7
  tors, 5, 24
  tourmaline, 34
gravel, 13
Greenland, 27
grinding stones, 33
Guilan Hills, 16
gypsum, 13, 34

H

hardness, Mohs' scale,
  34
Hawaii, 20
Hay Tor, 5
hematite, 35, 41
Himalayas, 8, 13

Stalagmite

I

Iceland, 20
igneous rock, 24-5, 27
Indonesia, 44
industrial minerals,
    46-7
insects, in amber, 15
Iraq, 40
iron, 25, 50
    hematite, 35
    meteorites, 52
Italy, 22

J

jade, 40, 41
jadeite, 40
Jerusalem, 30
jewelry, 40, 44-5

K

karst scenery, 16
kimberlite, 25
Kolo people, 38
Kwakiutl people, 33

L

labradorite, 31
landslides, 7, 10
lapis lazuli, 39, 40, 41
lava:
    amethyst, 36
    eruptions, 20, 22
    geodes, 43
    obsidian, 32
    oceanic crust, 9
    pumice, 23
lead ore, 35, 51
limestone:
    caves, 16-17
    cement, 31
    formation, 14
    fossils, 14, 29
    pavements, 16

M

marble, 28
    Mount Everest, 13
    nummulitic, 11
    limonite, 43
magma:
    amethyst, 36
    eruptions, 20, 23
    geodes, 43
    pipes, 25
    volcanic plugs, 4
malachite, 39
Maoris, 41
marble, 28-9, 30, 31
Mars, 52
Martinique, 23
Maya, 32

Medici family, 31
mercury, 50
Mesopotamia, 30
metals:
    ores, 50-1
    precious metals, 48-9
metamorphic rocks,
    26-7
    marble, 28-9
meteorites, 52-3
mica, 6
Michelangelo, 29
microline, 7
Mid-Atlantic Ridge, 9
Mohs' scale of hardness,
    34
Montserrat, 21
Moon, 52, 53
moonstone, 7
mortar, 31
mosaics, 30
mountains:
    formation, 6, 8-9
    metamorphic rocks, 27
mud:
    metamorphic rocks, 7,
        26

Labradorite

sedimentary rocks, 12
mudstone, 13, 26

N

nephrite, 40, 41
New Zealand, 21, 41
North American Indians, 39
nummulitic limestone, 11

O

obsidian, 32
oceanic plates, 9
ochre, 38
oil, 18
ores, metallic, 50-1
orthoclase feldspar, 7, 34

P

pahoehoe lava, 20
Pamukkale, 16

peat, 18
pegmatites, 24
Pelée, Mont, 23
Persians, 39
petrified wood, 19
petroleum, 18
pewter, 51
pigments, 38-9
pipes, volcanic, 25
plants, fossil fuels, 18
platinum, 48
potato stones, 43
precious metals, 48-9
prehistoric man:
    cave paintings, 38
    stone tools, 32-3
pumice, 23
Puy de Dôme, 4
pyrite, 37

Q

quartz, 42-3
    amethyst, 36
    geodes, 25
    granite, 7, 34
    hardness, 35

pegmatites, 24
petrified wood, 19
radios, 36
tiger's eye, 41
watches, 46

R

rain:
    acid rain, 10, 28
    erosion, 16
resin, 15
Rhône Glacier, 10
Rio de Janeiro, 25
rock cycle, 6
Romans, 30, 33, 38
rubies, 34, 44, 45, 46

S

St. Helens, Mount, 23
salt water, 13
San Andreas fault, 8
San Francisco, 8

sand:
    dunes, 12
    quartz, 42
    ripples, 4, 5
    sedimentary rocks, 12
sandstone, 12
sapphires, 44, 45
schist, 27
Scotland, 42
sculpture, 28, 29
sea creatures:
    chalk, 14
    limestone, 16

Quartz

Ruby boule

sedimentary rocks, 12-13
    fossils, 14-15
shale, 13, 26
shells, limestone, 14
Sicily, 22
silica, 32
silicon chips, 46, 47
silver, 48, 49, 51
slate, 26-7
Solar System, 52
South Africa, 44, 49
South America, 40
space, 52-3
sphinx, 11
Sri Lanka, 44
stalactites and stalagmites, 16, 17
stone tools, 32-3
Stromboli, 22
Sugar Loaf Mountain, 25
sulphur, 35
Sumerians, 40
sunstone, 41
synthetic minerals, 46-7

T

talc, 34, 47
tectonic plates, 8-9, 20
Thailand, 44
thunder eggs, 43
tiger's eye, 41
tiles, 30
till, 10
tin, 51
tools, stone, 32-3
topaz, 35, 37
tors, 5, 24
tourmaline, 7, 24, 34
trees:
    fossil fuels, 19
    resin, 15
turquoise, 39

U

ultramarine, 39
Ur, 40

V

Vesuvius, Mount, 22
volcanoes:
    amethysts, 36
    eruptions, 9, 20, 22-3
    geodes, 43
    lava, 20-1
    pipes, 25
    plugs, 4
    sulphur crystals, 35

W

Warrumbungles, 5
weathering, 10-11, 24, 27
wood, petrified, 19
wulfenite, 35

Z

zeolite, 21
zircon, 37